NUMBER TRACING WORKBOOK

Handwriting Practice and Pen Control
Activity Book for Kids
Ages 3-5

This Book Belongs To:

_____

\

_____

_____

Look for a FREE activity
book offer at the end of
this workbook!

COTTAGE
PATH
PRESS

Let's learn numbers!

ISBN: 9798425679123
© 2022 Cottage Path Press
Visit us online at www.CottagePathPress.com

Ready to have fun learning to write numbers?

This workbook is organized into three main sections:

Section 1: Numbers 0 to 20
Learn the basic numbers by tracing, spelling, and writing. Plenty of room to practice with two full pages of dotted line writing guides for each number!

Section 2: Numbers 21 to 100
Continue learning beyond the basic numbers by tracing, spelling, and writing all the way to one hundred!

Section 3: Fun activity pages to reinforce learning
Enhance the number tracing exercises with activity pages featuring numbers 1 through 20. Students will count and color familiar animals and objects, then trace, spell, and write the numbers to increase comprehension while having fun!

Bonus Pages
At the end of each section, students will find a fun coloring page with an encouraging message praising their hard work. The final coloring page is also suitable as a certificate of completion for the book!

 Parents and teachers, look for a **FREE activity book** offer from Cottage Path Press at the end of this workbook!

zero

zero

zero

Practice tracing the number.

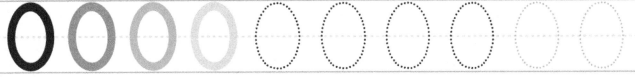

Now practice writing the number in the lines below.

Good job! Turn the page to practice some more.

Bee-utiful work!

one

one

one

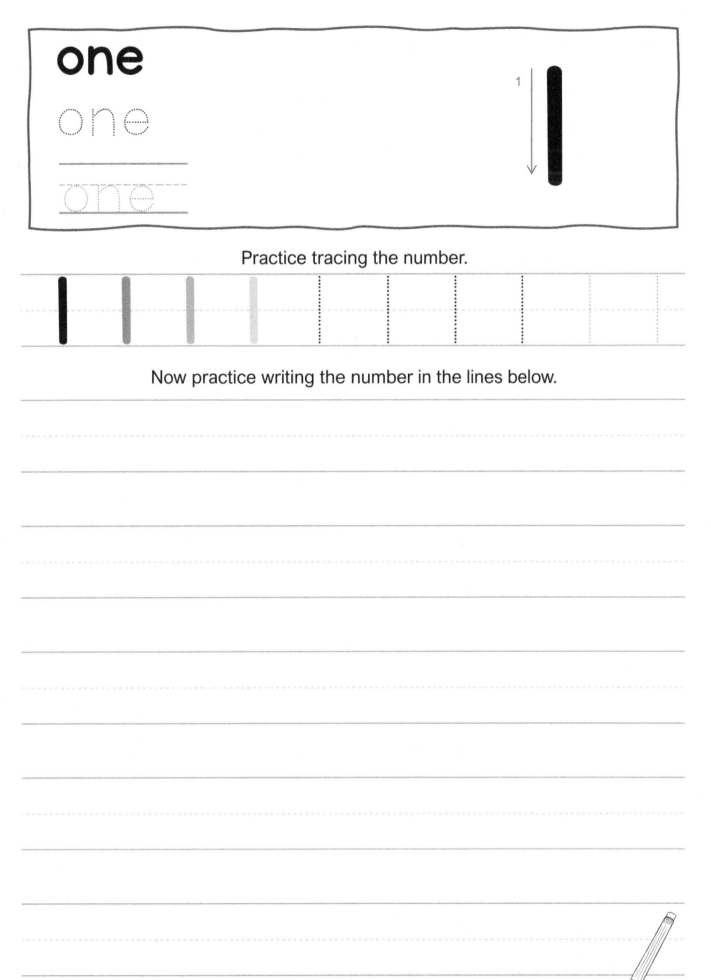

Practice tracing the number.

Now practice writing the number in the lines below.

Good job! Turn the page to practice some more.

Bee-utiful work!

two

two

two

2

Practice tracing the number.

2 2 2 2 2 2 2 2 2 2

Now practice writing the number in the lines below.

Good job! Turn the page to practice some more.

2 2 2 2 2 2 2 2 2 2

Bee-utiful work!

three

three

three

Practice tracing the number.

3 3 3 3 3 3 3 3 3 3

Now practice writing the number in the lines below.

Good job! Turn the page to practice some more.

3 3 3 3 3 3 3 3 3 3

Bee-utiful work!

four

four

four

Practice tracing the number.

4 4 4 4 4 4 4 4 4 4

Now practice writing the number in the lines below.

Good job! Turn the page to practice some more.

4 4 4 4 4 4 4 4 4

Bee-utiful work!

five

five

five

Practice tracing the number.

5 5 5 5 5 5 5 5 5 5

Now practice writing the number in the lines below.

Good job! Turn the page to practice some more.

5 5 5 5 5 5 5 5 5 5

Bee-utiful work!

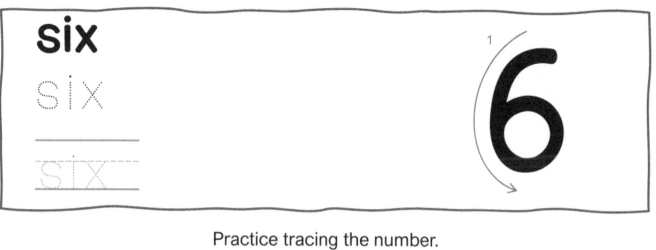

six

six

six

6

Practice tracing the number.

6 6 6 6 6 6 6 6 6 6

Now practice writing the number in the lines below.

Good job! Turn the page to practice some more.

Bee-utiful work!

seven

seven

_____

seven

7 ₂
1 →

Practice tracing the number.

7 7 7 7 7 7 7 7 7

Now practice writing the number in the lines below.

Good job! Turn the page to practice some more.

7 7 7 7 7 7 7 7 7

Bee-utiful work!

eight

eight

eight

Practice tracing the number.

8 8 8 8 8 8 8 8 8 8

Now practice writing the number in the lines below.

Good job! Turn the page to practice some more.

Bee-utiful work!

nine

nine

nine

nine

q

1

2

Practice tracing the number.

q q q q q q q q q q q q

Now practice writing the number in the lines below.

Good job! Turn the page to practice some more.

q q q q q q q q q q q q

Bee-utiful work!

ten

ten

ten

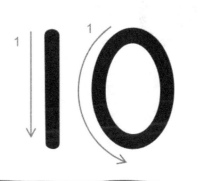

Practice tracing the number.

10 10 10 10 10 10 10

Now practice writing the number in the lines below.

Good job! Turn the page to practice some more.

10 10 10 10 10 10 10

Bee-utiful work!

eleven

eleven

eleven

Practice tracing the number.

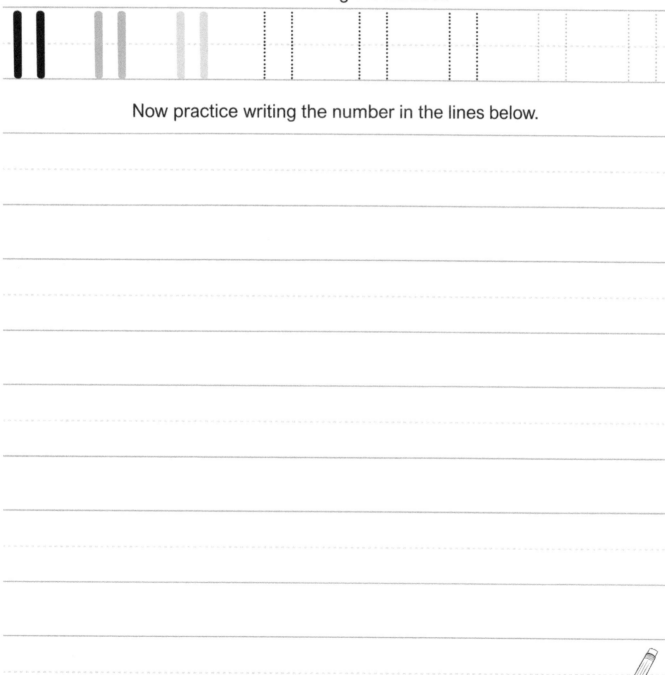

Now practice writing the number in the lines below.

Good job! Turn the page to practice some more.

Bee-utiful work!

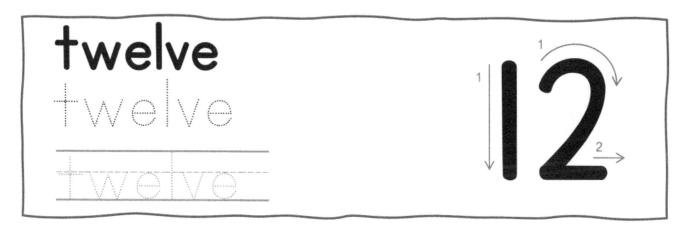

twelve

Practice tracing the number.

Now practice writing the number in the lines below.

12 12 12 12 12 12 12 12

Bee-utiful work!

thirteen

thirteen

thirteen

Practice tracing the number.

13 13 13 13 13 13 13 13

Now practice writing the number in the lines below.

Good job! Turn the page to practice some more.

13 13 13 13 13 13 13 13

Bee-utiful work!

fourteen

fourteen

fourteen

Practice tracing the number.

14 14 14 14 14 14 14 14

Now practice writing the number in the lines below.

Good job! Turn the page to practice some more.

14 14 14 14 14 14 14 14

Bee-utiful work!

fifteen

fifteen

fifteen

15

Practice tracing the number.

15 15 15 15 15 15 15 15

Now practice writing the number in the lines below.

Good job! Turn the page to practice some more.

15 15 15 15 15 15 15 15

Bee-utiful work!

sixteen

sixteen

sixteen

1↓ 1 16

Practice tracing the number.

16 16 16 16 16 16 16 16

Now practice writing the number in the lines below.

Good job! Turn the page to practice some more.

16 16 16 16 16 16 16 16

Bee-utiful work!

seventeen

seventeen

seventeen

1 ⟶
1 **17** 2

Practice tracing the number.

17 17 17 17 17 17 17 17

Now practice writing the number in the lines below.

Good job! Turn the page to practice some more.

Bee-utiful work!

eighteen
eighteen

eighteen

Practice tracing the number.

18 18 18 18 18 18 18 18

Now practice writing the number in the lines below.

Good job! Turn the page to practice some more.

18 18 18 18 18 18 18 18

Bee-utiful work!

nineteen

nineteen

nineteen

19

Practice tracing the number.

19 19 19 19 19 19 19 19

Now practice writing the number in the lines below.

Good job! Turn the page to practice some more.

19 19 19 19 19 19 19

Bee-utiful work!

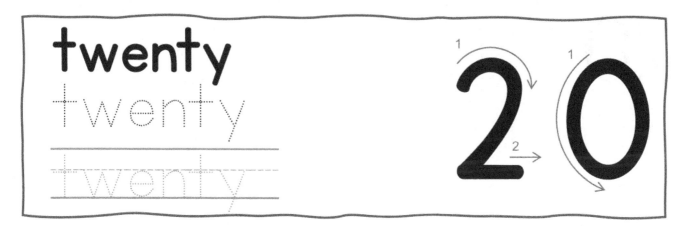

twenty

twenty

twenty

Practice tracing the number.

20 20 20 20 20 20

Now practice writing the number in the lines below.

Good job! Turn the page to practice some more.

20 20 20 20 20 20

Bee-utiful work!

Woo-hoo! You are doing a great job!
Have fun coloring this page to celebrate your good work.

You
are
amazing!

twenty-one

twenty-one

twenty-one

Practice tracing the number.

21 21 21 21 21 21 21 21

Now practice writing the number on the line below.

twenty-two

twenty-two

twenty-two

22 22

Practice tracing the number.

22 22 22 22 22 22

Now practice writing the number on the line below.

twenty-three

twenty-three

twenty-three

2 3

Practice tracing the number.

23 23 23 23 23 23

Now practice writing the number on the line below.

twenty-four

twenty-four

twenty-four

2 4

Practice tracing the number.

24 24 24 24 24

Now practice writing the number on the line below.

twenty-five

twenty-five

twenty-five

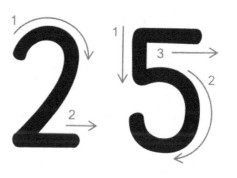

Practice tracing the number.

25 25 25 25 25 25

Now practice writing the number on the line below.

twenty-six

twenty-six

twenty-six

2 6

Practice tracing the number.

26 26 26 26 26 26

Now practice writing the number on the line below.

twenty-seven

twenty-seven

twenty-seven

Practice tracing the number.

27 27 27 27 27 27 27

Now practice writing the number on the line below.

twenty-eight

twenty-eight

twenty-eight

Practice tracing the number.

28 28 28 28 28 28

Now practice writing the number on the line below.

twenty-nine

twenty-nine

twenty-nine

Practice tracing the number.

29 29 29 29 29

Now practice writing the number on the line below.

thirty

thirty

thirty

Practice tracing the number.

30 30 30 30 30

Now practice writing the number on the line below.

thirty-one

thirty-one

thirty-one

Practice tracing the number.

3 1   3 1   3 1   3 1   3 1

Now practice writing the number on the line below.

thirty-two

thirty-two

thirty-two

Practice tracing the number.

3 2   3 2   3 2   3 2   3 2

Now practice writing the number on the line below.

thirty-three

thirty-three

thirty-three

3 3

Practice tracing the number.

33 33 33 33 33

Now practice writing the number on the line below.

thirty-four

thirty-four

thirty-four

3 4

Practice tracing the number.

34 34 34 34 34

Now practice writing the number on the line below.

thirty-five

thirty-five

thirty-five

Practice tracing the number.

35   35   35   35   35

Now practice writing the number on the line below.

thirty-six

thirty-six

thirty-six

Practice tracing the number.

36   36   36   36   36

Now practice writing the number on the line below.

thirty-seven

Practice tracing the number.

37 37 37 37 37 37

Now practice writing the number on the line below.

thirty-eight

Practice tracing the number.

38 38 38 38 38 38

Now practice writing the number on the line below.

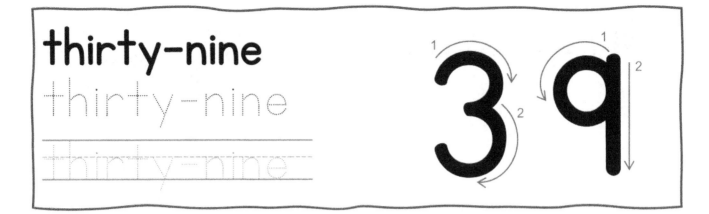

thirty-nine

thirty-nine

thirty-nine

Practice tracing the number.

39 39 39 39 39

Now practice writing the number on the line below.

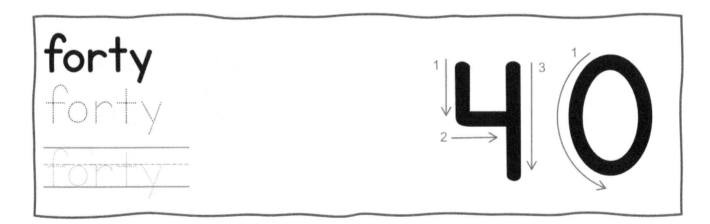

forty

forty

forty

Practice tracing the number.

40 40 40 40 40

Now practice writing the number on the line below.

forty-one

forty-one

forty-one

Practice tracing the number.

Now practice writing the number on the line below.

forty-two

forty-two

forty-two

Practice tracing the number.

Now practice writing the number on the line below.

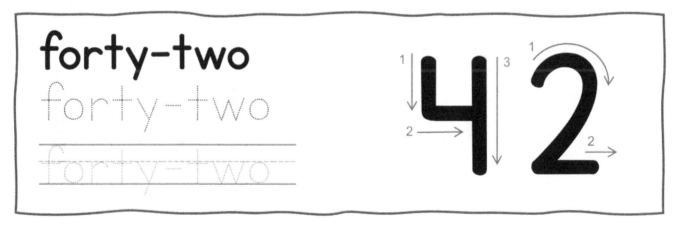

forty-three

forty-three

forty-three

Practice tracing the number.

43

Now practice writing the number on the line below.

forty-four

forty-four

forty-four

Practice tracing the number.

44

Now practice writing the number on the line below.

forty-five

forty-five

forty-five

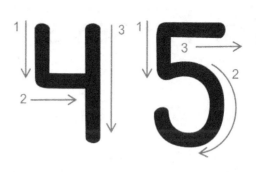

Practice tracing the number.

45 45 45 45 45

Now practice writing the number on the line below.

forty-six

forty-six

forty-six

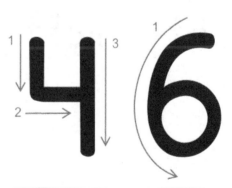

Practice tracing the number.

46 46 46 46 46

Now practice writing the number on the line below.

forty-seven

forty-seven

forty-seven

4 7

Practice tracing the number.

47   47   47   47   47

Now practice writing the number on the line below.

forty-eight

forty-eight

forty-eight

4 8

Practice tracing the number.

48   48   48   48   48

Now practice writing the number on the line below.

forty-nine

forty-nine

forty-nine

Practice tracing the number.

49

Now practice writing the number on the line below.

fifty

fifty

fifty

Practice tracing the number.

50

Now practice writing the number on the line below.

fifty-one

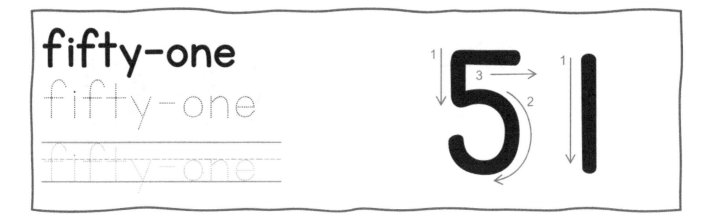

Practice tracing the number.

5 1 5 1 5 5 5 5 5

Now practice writing the number on the line below.

fifty-two

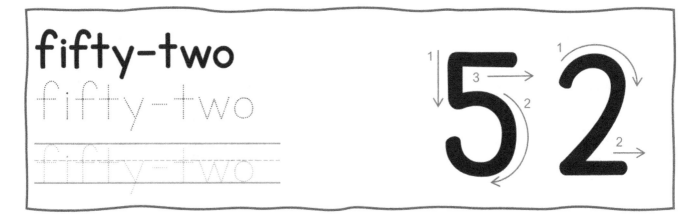

Practice tracing the number.

52 52 52 52 52 52

Now practice writing the number on the line below.

fifty-three

fifty-three

fifty-three

5 3

Practice tracing the number.

53 53 53 53 53 53

Now practice writing the number on the line below.

fifty-four

fifty-four

fifty-four

5 4

Practice tracing the number.

54 54 54 54 54 54

Now practice writing the number on the line below.

fifty-five

fifty-five

fifty-five

Practice tracing the number.

55 55 55 55 55

Now practice writing the number on the line below.

fifty-six

fifty-six

fifty-six

Practice tracing the number.

56 56 56 56 56

Now practice writing the number on the line below.

fifty-seven

Practice tracing the number.

57 57 57 57 57

Now practice writing the number on the line below.

fifty-eight

Practice tracing the number.

58 58 58 58 58

Now practice writing the number on the line below.

fifty-nine

Practice tracing the number.

59 59 59 59 59

Now practice writing the number on the line below.

sixty

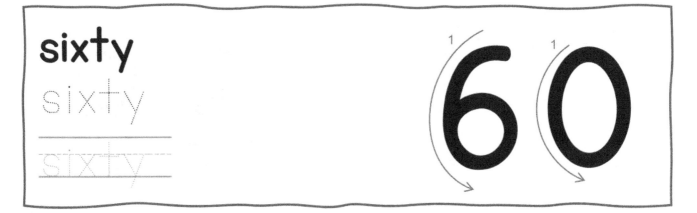

Practice tracing the number.

60 60 60 60 60

Now practice writing the number on the line below.

sixty-one

sixty-one

sixty-one

6 **1**

Practice tracing the number.

6 1 6 1 6 1 6 1 6 1

Now practice writing the number on the line below.

sixty-two

sixty-two

sixty-two

6 **2**

Practice tracing the number.

62 62 62 62 62

Now practice writing the number on the line below.

sixty-three

sixty-three

sixty-three

Practice tracing the number.

63   63   63   63   63   63   63

Now practice writing the number on the line below.

sixty-four

sixty-four

sixty-four

Practice tracing the number.

64   64   64   64   64   64

Now practice writing the number on the line below.

sixty-five

sixty-five

sixty-five

65

Practice tracing the number.

65 65 65 65 65 65

Now practice writing the number on the line below.

sixty-six

sixty-six

sixty-six

66

Practice tracing the number.

66 66 66 66 66 66

Now practice writing the number on the line below.

sixty-seven

sixty-seven

Practice tracing the number.

67   67   67   67   67

Now practice writing the number on the line below.

sixty-eight

sixty-eight

sixty-eight

Practice tracing the number.

68   68   68   68   68

Now practice writing the number on the line below.

sixty-nine

sixty-nine

sixty-nine

Practice tracing the number.

69 69 69 69 69

Now practice writing the number on the line below.

seventy

seventy

seventy

Practice tracing the number.

70 70 70 70 70

Now practice writing the number on the line below.

seventy-one

seventy-one

seventy-one

7 1

Practice tracing the number.

71   7 1   7 1   7 1   7 1

Now practice writing the number on the line below.

seventy-two

seventy-two

seventy-two

7 2

Practice tracing the number.

72   72   72   72   72

Now practice writing the number on the line below.

seventy-three

seventy-three

seventy-three

7 3

Practice tracing the number.

73 73 73 73 73

Now practice writing the number on the line below.

seventy-four

seventy-four

seventy-four

7 4

Practice tracing the number.

74 74 74 74 74

Now practice writing the number on the line below.

seventy-five

seventy-five

seventy-five

Practice tracing the number.

75 75 75 75 75 75

Now practice writing the number on the line below.

seventy-six

seventy-six

seventy-six

Practice tracing the number.

76 76 76 76 76 76

Now practice writing the number on the line below.

seventy-seven

seventy-seven

seventy-seven

Practice tracing the number.

77 77 77 77 77 77

Now practice writing the number on the line below.

seventy-eight

seventy-eight

seventy-eight

Practice tracing the number.

78 78 78 78 78

Now practice writing the number on the line below.

seventy-nine

seventy-nine

seventy-nine

7 9

Practice tracing the number.

7 9   7 9   7 9   7 9   7 9

Now practice writing the number on the line below.

eighty

eighty

eighty

8 0

Practice tracing the number.

80   80   80   80   80

Now practice writing the number on the line below.

eighty-one

eighty-one

eighty-one

8 1

Practice tracing the number.

8 1   8 1   8 1   8 1   8 1   8 1

Now practice writing the number on the line below.

eighty-two

eighty-two

eighty-two

8 2

Practice tracing the number.

8 2   8 2   8 2   8 2   8 2

Now practice writing the number on the line below.

eighty-three

eighty-three

eighty-three

Practice tracing the number.

83 83 83 83 83

Now practice writing the number on the line below.

eighty-four

eighty-four

eighty-four

Practice tracing the number.

84 84 84 84 84

Now practice writing the number on the line below.

eighty-five

eighty-five

eighty-five

Practice tracing the number.

85 85 85 85 85

Now practice writing the number on the line below.

eighty-six

eighty-six

eighty-six

Practice tracing the number.

86 86 86 86 86

Now practice writing the number on the line below.

eighty-seven

eighty-seven

eighty-seven

Practice tracing the number.

87 87 87 87 87

Now practice writing the number on the line below.

eighty-eight

eighty-eight

eighty-eight

Practice tracing the number.

88 88 88 88 88

Now practice writing the number on the line below.

eighty-nine

eighty-nine

eighty-nine

Practice tracing the number.

8 9   8 9   8 9   8 9   8 9

Now practice writing the number on the line below.

ninety

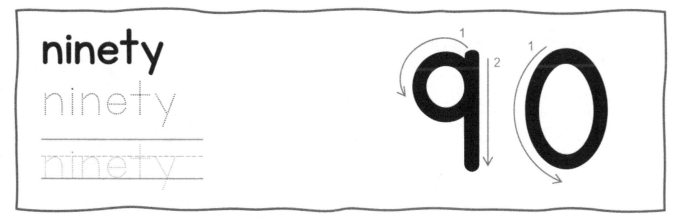

ninety

ninety

Practice tracing the number.

9 0   9 0   9 0   9 0   9 0

Now practice writing the number on the line below.

ninety-one

ninety-one

ninety-one

Practice tracing the number.

91   91   91   91   91   91   91

Now practice writing the number on the line below.

ninety-two

ninety-two

ninety-two

Practice tracing the number.

92   92   92   92   92   92

Now practice writing the number on the line below.

ninety-three

ninety-three

ninety-three

93

Practice tracing the number.

93   93   93   93   93

Now practice writing the number on the line below.

ninety-four

ninety-four

ninety-four

94

Practice tracing the number.

94   94   94   94   94

Now practice writing the number on the line below.

ninety-five

ninety-five

ninety-five

Practice tracing the number.

95   95   95   95   95

Now practice writing the number on the line below.

ninety-six

ninety-six

ninety-six

Practice tracing the number.

96   96   96   96   96

Now practice writing the number on the line below.

ninety-seven

ninety-seven

ninety-seven

9 7

Practice tracing the number.

97 97 97 97 97

Now practice writing the number on the line below.

ninety-eight

ninety-eight

ninety-eight

9 8

Practice tracing the number.

98 98 98 98 98

Now practice writing the number on the line below.

ninety-nine

ninety-nine

ninety-nine

9 9

Practice tracing the number.

9 9 9 9 9 9 9 9 9 9

Now practice writing the number on the line below.

one hundred

one hundred

one hundred

100

Practice tracing the number.

100 100 100 100

Now practice writing the number on the line below.

Wow! You are a superstar student!
Have fun coloring this page to celebrate how much you've learned.

Count and Color

I dog

Practice tracing the letters.

one one one one

Now write the word on your own.

Practice tracing and writing the number.

| |

Circle just **one** bone.

Count and Color

2 cats

Practice tracing the letters.

two two two two

Now write the word on your own.

Practice tracing and writing the number.

2 2 2 2

Circle just **two** cat beds.

Count and Color

3 unicorns

Practice tracing the letters.

three three three

Now write the word on your own.

Practice tracing and writing the number.

3 3 3 3

Circle just **three** rainbows.

Count and Color

4 squirrels

Practice tracing the letters.

four four four four

Now write the word on your own.

Practice tracing and writing the number.

4 4 4 4

Circle just **four** acorns.

Count and Color
5 racecars

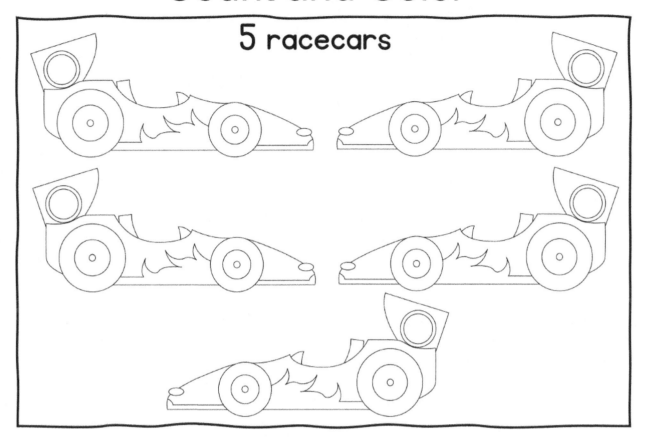

Practice tracing the letters.

five five five five

Now write the word on your own.

Practice tracing and writing the number.

5 5 5 5

Circle just **five** trophies.

Count and Color

6 glue bottles

GLUE GLUE GLUE

GLUE GLUE GLUE

Practice tracing the letters.

six six six six six

Now write the word on your own.

Practice tracing and writing the number.

6 6 6 6

Circle just **six** scissors.

Count and Color
7 hot dogs

Practice tracing the letters.

seven seven seven

Now write the word on your own.

Practice tracing and writing the number.

7 7 7 7

Circle just **seven** burgers.

Count and Color

8 dinosaurs

Practice tracing the letters.

eight eight eight

Now write the word on your own.

Practice tracing and writing the number.

8 8 8 8

Circle just **eight** dinosaur eggs.

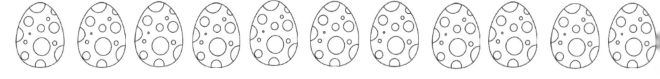

Count and Color

9 owls

Practice tracing the letters.

nine nine nine nine

Now write the word on your own.

Practice tracing and writing the number.

q q q q

Circle just **nine** trees.

Count and Color

10 rabbits

Practice tracing the letters.

ten ten ten ten ten

Now write the word on your own.

Practice tracing and writing the number.

10 10 10 10

Circle just **ten** carrots.

Count and Color
ll backpacks

Practice tracing the letters.

eleven eleven eleven

Now write the word on your own.

Practice tracing and writing the number.

ll

Circle just **eleven** books.

Count and Color

12 seahorses

Practice tracing the letters.

twelve twelve twelve

Now write the word on your own.

Practice tracing and writing the number.

12 12 12 12

Circle just **twelve** shells.

Count and Color

13 trumpets

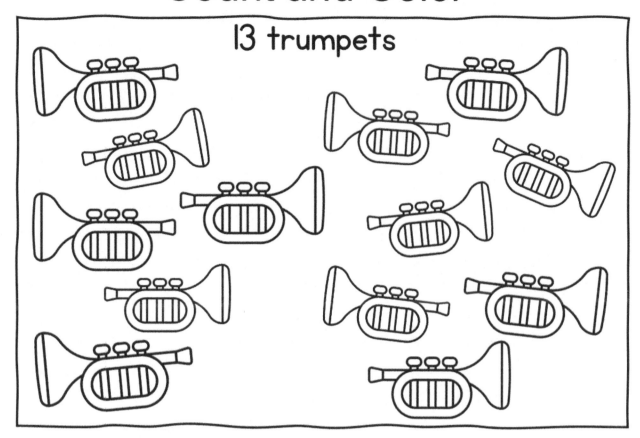

Practice tracing the letters.

thirteen ‌thirteen

Now write the word on your own.

Practice tracing and writing the number.

13 13 13 13

Circle just **thirteen** musical notes.

Count and Color

14 rockets

Practice tracing the letters.

fourteen fourteen

Now write the word on your own.

Practice tracing and writing the number.

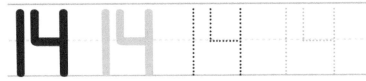

Circle just **fourteen** stars.

Count and Color

15 monkeys

Practice tracing the letters.

fifteen fifteen

Now write the word on your own.

Practice tracing and writing the number.

15 15 15 15

Circle just **fifteen** bananas.

Count and Color

16 snowmen

Practice tracing the letters.

sixteen sixteen

Now write the word on your own.

Practice tracing and writing the number.

16 16 16 16

Circle just **sixteen** snowflakes.

Count and Color

17 umbrellas

Practice tracing the letters.

seventeen seventeen

Now write the word on your own.

Practice tracing and writing the number.

17 17 17 17

Circle just **seventeen** raindrops.

0 0 0 0 0 0 0 0 0 0 0 0 0 0 0 0 0 0

Count and Color

18 leaves

Practice tracing the letters.

eighteen eighteen

Now write the word on your own.

Practice tracing and writing the number.

18 18 18 18

Circle just **eighteen** rakes.

Count and Color

19 notebooks

Practice tracing the letters.

nineteen nineteen

Now write the word on your own.

Practice tracing and writing the number.

19 19 19 19

Circle just **nineteen** pencils.

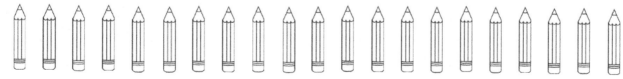

Count and Color

20 flower pots

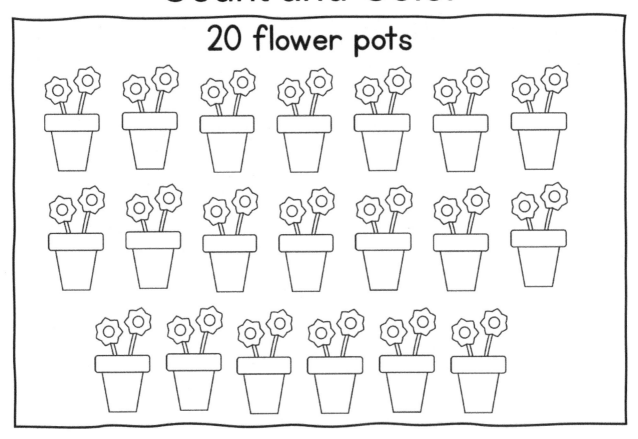

Practice tracing the letters.

twenty twenty

Now write the word on your own.

Practice tracing and writing the number.

20 20 20 20

Circle just **twenty** flowers.

Bee proud of all your AWESOME work!

Thank you for purchasing
this book!

We appreciate your trust in us!
Cottage Path Press is a small, U.S. family business. As parents (and grandparents) ourselves, we strive to publish quality books that are not only entertaining and educational for little learners, but also fun to give or receive.

If you and your child enjoyed this book, we'd be so grateful if you'd take a moment to leave a review on Amazon.

We value your comments and we truly appreciate your support for our business!

BONUS BOOK!

Would you like a FREE tracing activity book for kids that you can download and print at home?

To get your copy, please visit the link below:

https://bit.ly/tracingbonusbook

Come see what's new from Cottage Path Press

Look for more of our fun and educational books for kids!

We also have great books for adults and seniors!

Search for us at Amazon or visit:

www.CottagePathPress.com

Made in United States
North Haven, CT
23 March 2022

17431115R00063